My Mate's Gone Mad!

My Mate's Gone Mad!

*Isn't Christianity Weird,
Irrelevant and Untrue?*

Graham Daniels

Series Editor Jonathan Carswell

Authentic

LONDON ● COLORADO SPRINGS ● HYDERABAD

First published 2007 by Authentic Media
9 Holdom Avenue, Bletchley, Milton Keynes, Bucks, MK1 1QR, UK
1820 Jet Stream Drive, Colorado Springs, CO 80921, USA
OM Authentic Media, Medchal Road, Jeedimetla Village, Secunderabad
500 055, A.P., India
www.authenticmedia.co.uk
Authentic Media is a division of IBS-STL U.K., limited by guarantee,
with its Registered Office at Kingstown Broadway, Carlisle, Cumbria
CA3 0HA. Registered in England & Wales No. 1216232.
Registered charity 270162

British Library Cataloguing in Publication Data
A catalogue record for this book is available from the
British Library

ISBN-13: 978-1-85078-764-8
ISBN-10: 1-85078-764-6

Cover Design by David McNeill
Print Management by Adare Carwin
Printed and bound in Great Britain by J.H. Haynes & Co., Sparkford

Introduction to the Exploring Christianity series

Rubbernecking. We've all done it, haven't we? Curiously and suspiciously having a nosey at something . . . keen to find out what's going on. Whether it's on the motorway with an accident on the other side; across a crowded street in town, as a man is arrested for shoplifting; or perhaps an elderly lady who has fainted is treated by paramedics. There is just something about finding out what all the fuss is about.

Perhaps that's why you've picked up this book. Christianity and the person of Jesus might be something you know very little about, but you've heard or seen something that makes you want to know more and so here you are . . .

This is just one of a series of short books written for people who are perhaps just starting to look at what Christianity is all about. We hope that through this series you'll be able to explore a little more and find out the facts for yourself.

So, your invite is here . . . come rubberneck with us as we look at the issue of who Jesus is and find the answer to 'Is He relevant today?' . . .

Jonathan Carswell
Series Editor

I took the one spare seat on the bus, right next to the skipper, Gwyon Jenkins

Isn't Christianity just weird?

'Daniels, go home and get your kit, you're playing this afternoon!'

Result! Alright, so it wasn't really on merit. My school's 1st XI was short of a few senior lads and they needed some younger kids to fill in. But who cares? A whole afternoon of cricket and even better, missing double maths and biology.

Our opponents were fifty miles away, just outside Cardiff and so very 'posh' to those of us living in the Wild, Wild West of Llanelli. In Wales though, being a posh school didn't necessarily make you any good. In fact, far from it in our opinion. We had a rather sophisticated rhyming couplet for the school we were playing on this particular day: **'All the gear but no idea!'**

Indeed, that proved to be the case on this particular occasion and we beat them soundly, the game finishing early. On leaving, I was last to return to the twelve-seater school minibus. The others kindly excused my pedestrian speed since, as I explained once on board, batting throughout the *whole* innings does necessitate a good long shower. . . I took the one spare seat on the bus, right next to the skipper, Gwyon Jenkins.

It was a long journey home and we hardly knew each other. Our conversation began with promising fluidity, ten minutes spent talking about the two flying catches taken at mid-off, the quality of our off-spinner and the speed with which we overtook our opponents' meagre total. Keeping the chat undemanding I asked if he played cricket at the weekend (this being a Monday). I was keeping the banter going about **the one thing that really mattered: sport**. He replied by telling me about his cricket match on Saturday. Fantastic. Now we were off and talking about mutual acquaintances that played in his team and a wide-ranging discussion ensued about their wicket keeping capacities, off drives and leg side weaknesses.

In due course, however, our discussion began to flag as quickly as our adversaries' middle order batsmen, the sure sign being that we had started padding out our conversation by talking about my O Levels and his A Levels. At this point, we both knew that our interaction was running out of steam and with it being summer and no rugby to talk about we had now exhausted any worthwhile subjects.

To shut up however, would have been awkward and there was no easy way of speaking to anyone else on the high seated minibus. British culture dictates that when you sit on a bus with a stranger or relative stranger you face a dilemma. It appears rude to ignore their existence but experience teaches you that this is actually the lesser of two evils if you maybe can't keep a conversation going for the whole journey. To start and then run out of conversation is dreadful to all concerned. So an initial two minutes' silence, staring out of the window may feel awkward but both you and your neighbour know that in the end it'll be less uncomfortable than starting talking and then trying desperately to keep going for fifty whole miles.

We had started now though, so we had to keep going – there were at least thirty miles to go.

I pitched in first, asking what Gwyon had done on his second rest day from school, namely Sunday. He replied that he had gone to church. What: to church? Don't panic, think rationally. Gwyon Jenkins was in the Upper Sixth. I failed; my brain was scrambled so I blurted out the first thing that came to mind. 'Does your mother still make you go to Sunday School at the age of eighteen?' Oh you idiot, what a stupid and rude thing to say.

Then it got worse; yes, worse. Instead of cringing deeply at my inappropriate response, he answered gently, calmly and with clarity that *he* chose to go to church because he was a Christian. Oh no! **Thirty miles to go and my worst fears are realised. I'm sitting next to a Bible Basher**, with no alternative seat and travelling down the motorway at sixty miles an hour. Frankly, I can't remember what on earth actually happened between us for the next half an hour but even now I'm perspiring at the thought. My brain must have pushed it as far away from my consciousness as possible since it was clearly a very traumatic experience.

Thirty miles to go and my **worst fears** are realised. I'm sitting **next to a Bible Basher**

All I can remember thinking (as opposed to saying) was 'How could this be?' This guy was normal. No, even more, he was cool. He was a good sportsman and could even have a laugh. But he was a Christian. Brain ache.

After the fateful journey home on that early Monday evening, my instinct was to avoid him in the same way I'd avoid someone with the flu or someone from Swansea. However, now that I was playing cricket for the school team that was impossible. Worse still, it transpired that his girlfriend lived in my village. From not knowing him at all, I was now seeing him two or three times a week. And guess what: he was a really good lad. Really normal in the important ways, the things that really mattered; which of course meant he played cricket, rugby and football, supported Llanelli Rugby Club, Liverpool Football Club and had a girlfriend.

Meeting and getting to know Gwyon Jenkins was the beginning of a seven year process for me where, in retrospect, I crossed the first of three barriers that were blocking my path to a life-changing experience. In due course I understood, experienced and entered into a restored relationship with the God who made the universe and made me to worship and enjoy Him both now and forever. And even as I re-read that sentence I can imagine you thinking, 'Oh no! He turned into a weirdo too.'

Well, the relief for you is that you're not trapped on a minibus next to me with thirty miles to go; instead you're reading it in a book and probably doing so in the most private place possible so that no one, neither Bernard the Bible Basher nor Normal Neil your best mate will spot you enquiring about Christianity. Just in case though, have a quick look behind you, since you can never be sure.

I wonder, though, who gave you this little book. He or she may not be called Gwyon (I think there's probably only one 'Gwyon' in the world) but I'm sure that person will be very much like him, unless of course she's a girl then there will be one or two critical differences. The main similarity will be that having got to know this friend you will have discovered that they are a follower of Jesus Christ and are reasonably normal. At first it's quite a hard thing to grasp, isn't it? On the other hand don't you find it a little intriguing, even exciting – yet at the same time scary? If they can be a Christian and they are quite like you (normal), that means that someone like you could be a Christian . . .

Are you willing to come along with me as we explore the Christian faith? If so, think of this part of the Gwyon story as the first of three barriers to getting to the heart of the Christian message. The 'weird' barrier is one you've just begun to cross over, and that's a pretty universal experience in coming to understand Jesus.

In the first chapter of John's account of the life of Jesus* we come across two friends who get into an unexpected conversation about Jesus. As we trace the story through we can see how the one who had already met Jesus,

*John was someone who followed Jesus and His work closely – sometimes called a disciple.

If they can be a Christian and they are **quite like you (normal),** that means that someone like you **could be a Christian . . .**

namely **Philip, helped his friend Nathanael overcome these three barriers to faith**. Let's have a look at the story in John chapter 1 v 43–51 and begin specifically with the first part of that story, recorded in verses 43-46.

> *The next day Jesus decided to leave for Galilee. Finding Philip, he said to him, "Follow me."*
>
> *Philip, like Andrew and Peter, was from the town of Bethsaida. Philip found Nathanael and told him, "We have found the one Moses wrote about in the Law, and about whom the prophets also wrote— Jesus of Nazareth, the son of Joseph."*
>
> *"Nazareth! Can anything good come from there?" Nathanael asked.*

As we join the story Jesus has just started to make Himself known in public and is in the process of inviting people to be members of His team, called by John His disciples. On the day before the incident we are looking at here,[1] Jesus had 'signed on' three disciples. Now in verse 43 He gives Philip the invitation to 'Follow me.' There were now four disciples from the same town, Bethsaida, and one of them, Philip, goes to find Nathanael to pass on the exciting news.[2]

[1] v35-42 [2] v45

Picture the chat if you can. Presuming they were typical mates it might have gone like this: 'Good Morning Nat!' 'Alright Phil, how are things?' 'Great, mate. Guess who I've met today! *The one Moses wrote about in the Law, and about whom the prophets also wrote—Jesus of Nazareth, the son of Joseph.*'[3]

To understand what he means here it's worth pointing out at this stage that these two guys were Jews. This matters because the Jewish nation had been yearning for a Jewish King who would rescue them from their enemies for around six hundred years. He had been promised in the Jewish Scriptures; known to Christians as the Old Testament. He had been promised by two of the great authorities of those Scriptures, namely Moses and the prophets. So when Philip tells Nathanael that he had met 'the one Moses wrote about in the Law, and about whom the prophets also wrote' he was making a rather bold claim. After six hundred years of waiting, the King of the Jews had appeared to his mate Philip on a normal working day in Israel.

Try and imagine the madness of such a claim from Nathanael's point of view. Here? Now? To Phil from number 22 down the road, whom I've known since primary school? Nathanael might have reasoned that it was a hot country so perhaps Philip had been in the sun too long that day. Perhaps work had been stressful, or things at home had not been so great. Pity, something must have toppled him over the edge towards such madness.

[3] v45

His final comment in this rush of claims is that this King is '*Jesus of Nazareth, the son of Joseph.*'[4] Now he knows his mate really *has* gone mad! This is a step too far for Nathanael. They may know each other well, but at this point his incredulity towards Philip's report spills over. '"*Nazareth! Can anything good come from there?*" *Nathanael asked*.'[5] Nazareth was a tiny village in their own region, but one never even mentioned in the Jewish Scriptures. Indeed, every Jew knew from their Bible that the King of the Jews would come from Bethlehem, as specifically foretold by one of their prophets Micah.[6] Bethlehem and Nazareth were a long way apart, one at the northern end and the other at the southern end of the country, they could not be confused.

So it appears that the only thing keeping Nathanael from just ignoring Philip completely was that he knew him. Had he not he would surely have surveyed the situation and said to himself 'He's a nutter!' and either called an ambulance, the police or run away. But here's the key issue. Philip and Nathanael *did* know each other. So often the good news about Jesus is passed on from one to another through a friend. This is important because the first impression of most people about Jesus is that the whole thing is weird. It's only because Nathanael knows him that he gives him the benefit of the doubt. Had he been a stranger, the conversation would have been over. **What Philip is talking about is all very weird, but Philip *isn't*, so his mate sticks in there for a moment longer**.

What Philip is talking about is **all very weird**, but Philip *isn't*, so his mate sticks in there for **a moment longer.**

Philip's lightness of touch is found by the way he partially rescues the situation. Notice how calm he is when Nathanael responds with vehemence at the suggestion that the King is from Nazareth: '*Nazareth, can anything good come from there?*' He could have taken offence at the strength of Nathanael's response. Why should his friend distrust his claim so strongly? He could have walked off in a huff, or answered with equal force. It's so easy to respond badly to someone's aggressive questioning. This is what's so great about Philip. He knows he's seen Jesus, he's confident that his analysis is correct and he knows he can introduce his friend to Him immediately. He is so secure in what he has discovered that he can offer the most understated and disarming of replies: '*Come and see*'.[7] The result, as we shall see in a moment, is that Nathanael does go to see.

Before we move on though, let's acknowledge that **very often the claims of Christianity may seem weird to someone who has heard them second or third hand**. That's why it is so revolutionary and incisive when a personal acquaintance or a friend meets Jesus. This is someone you know. Now, of course, there is the slight problem that your friend who becomes a follower of Jesus may actually be weird. However, it's to be hoped that this may be alleviated by the fact that they were weird before they became a Christian and that it wasn't coming to follow Jesus that was responsible.

[7] v46

Nathanael has overcome the weird barrier thanks to the fact that his friend has become a Christian. Despite Nathanael's protests about his claims, Philip offers his friend the chance to take a concrete, challenging but equally non-threatening step. He's offering the chance to verify his own claim – come and have a look. **There really is an actual man to meet behind what appears to be his sun-baked madness**. Thankfully, Philip's not been heavy-handed.

The result is that Nathanael goes to see Jesus: *'When Jesus saw Nathanael approaching . . . '*[8] Terrific! His friend has been 'first class' in his sensible approach, but it is still a very brave thing for Nathanael to do, making a move to check out this new King. A person has to be brave enough to reach out into the unknown and explore a relationship with Jesus Christ.

As you read this story, I wonder who you know as a 'follower of Jesus' – a Christian. If you've got this far you must at least have enough respect for them to take their claims seriously enough to explore their belief in Jesus personally? Good for you! **One barrier down, two to go to get to the heart of what a relationship with Jesus involves**.

One barrier down, **two to go . . .** to get to the heart **of what a relationship** with Jesus involves.

Christianity may not be weird, but it's surely irrelevant?

> *When Jesus saw Nathanael approaching, he said of him, "Here is a true Israelite, in whom there is nothing false."*
>
> *"How do you know me?" Nathanael asked.*
>
> *Jesus answered, "I saw you while you were still under the fig tree before Philip called you."*
>
> *Then Nathanael declared, "Rabbi, you are the Son of God, you are the King of Israel."*

So Jesus and Nathanael meet . . .

If Philip was wise in his approach to Nathanael, Jesus was brilliant! His 'Hello' is to say, '*Here is an Israelite in whom there is nothing false.*'[9] To us, this is meaningless, but there are two things worth noting that made a big difference to Nathanael. Firstly, Jesus is quoting the Jewish Scriptures, the language and literature of the faith which was the foundation of Nathanael's whole life and upbringing. It is a quote from the song book used when Jews gathered together for public worship. In the hymn in question, called a Psalm,[10] the writer tells of his yearning to be in a right relationship with God – **his desire more than anything else in the world is to overcome his own shortcomings, his sin against God**. The second thing that's important to Nathanael is that Jesus takes the initiative in starting the conversation.

[9] v47   [10] ch32 v2

In quoting the ancient hymn he's grown up with, Jesus breaks right through to Nathanael's deepest hopes. He shocks him. How on earth, muses Nathanael, can a man who I've never met before quote a song to me that is a perfect summary of everything I feel and hope for? How can this stranger know my most private emotions? Where is this guy taking me?

He starts the conversation by quoting this particular Psalm and the reason why Jesus takes the initiative is immediately apparent. Nathanael is stunned at such a perceptive, insightful comment on Jesus' part and responds, '*How do you know me?*'[11] The weird barrier fell earlier – now Jesus is beginning to breach the defence of the next barrier to often hinder the understanding of His message – that Christianity is irrelevant.

Jesus hadn't finished yet. '*I saw you when you were still under the fig tree before Philip called you.*'[12] Again, let's understand this response in its original context. Nathanael *may* have been sheltering from the shade of the sun when his friend showed up on this particular day. But Jesus had much more in mind than that. He's ensuring that Nathanael no longer has any doubt that **Jesus really does understand his heart**; that He empathises with what really resonates with his soul.

He is re-enforcing this for Nathanael by repeating what He's done earlier in the conversation, taking a portion of

[11] v48   [12] v48

the Scriptures he had grown up with and quoting a section that was completely harmonious with the kind of dreams Nathanael nurtured privately. The Jews believed the day would come when their promised king would restore the land of Israel to them. To sit under the fig tree in the noon-day sun was, according the prophet Zechariah[13] a privilege that would arrive for the male head of every Jewish family when that great day came. On that day, the head of his family would farm his own family's land, not leased by another or by an occupying nation. It would be a day of dignity, a sure sign that their king had been victorious.

This was then the utopian dream of Israel and Jesus clearly identified that it was the utopian dream of Nathanael himself. The dream of the day when the nation's Saviour would defeat the current occupying force, the Romans, and liberate his Jewish nation from oppression.

Can you see what's happening? The focus of the conversation has moved from the weirdness of Philip's claim about having met the King of Israel. It has moved from a third person witness to a personal and existential experience on the part of Nathanael. Somehow this stranger he has just met knows more about him than could possibly be imagined. How on earth can he?

We're getting close to the collapse of the irrelevant barrier. The focus of the conversation is moving towards Nathanael's discovery that to meet King Jesus is to encounter something and indeed someone that is far from

We're getting close to the collapse of the irrelevant barrier merely objective and distant. To meet this King is to have one's inner feelings and motivations exposed. This King knows what he feels and who he is. He knows Nathanael's hopes, dreams and so no doubt his fears too. He empathises with a man who dreams of a better world for himself and his children. **He dreams of a world where justice and fairness are restored, a world of liberation and hope to replace a bitterly unjust rule over his nation and his family – wouldn't we all?**

The result of this unexpected meeting with Jesus is that Nathanael's view is entirely changed. His attitude to Philip's friend is radically altered, displayed in his response to Jesus: '*Rabbi, you are the Son of God, you are the King of Israel.*'[14] It's barely five minutes since he was saying to his friend, '*Nazareth, can anything good come from there?*' He's now calling the very same man 'Rabbi', a term of authority accredited to a Jewish leader – and a major step towards respecting this stranger, acknowledging that this 'Teacher' does have authority and therefore something to say.

There were many rabbis in Israel though and Nathanael does more than just acknowledge that Jesus is your 'bog-standard' Jewish rabbi. Nathanael goes as far as it is possible to go in granting a leader status. You're 'the Son of God' and 'the King of Israel', Nathanael says. There could only be one such man and he's confirming Philip's initial assessment that Jesus is '*the one Moses wrote about in the Law and about whom the prophets also wrote—Jesus of Nazareth the son of Joseph*'.[15]

[14] v49 [15] v45

25

What a turnaround! He now accepts that **believing in Jesus is neither weird nor irrelevant**. Jesus understands Nathanael's hopes and dreams, and has empathy with him. Nathanael is most certainly prepared to commit to follow this Rabbi, the man he calls the 'the King of Israel'. On one level we have surely come to the climax of the story? Jesus has seen the sceptic persuaded, the cynic convinced. The natural move now would perhaps be for Nathanael himself to go find his friends and tell them what he now knows and has staked his future on. It would appear the obvious and congruent conclusion to the story, wouldn't it?

Like many who come to faith in Jesus Christ as a young adult, I can remember the thrill of beginning to understand that Jesus was interested in *me*. This is the most crucial change of perspective in coming to see how vibrant and purposeful it is to trust in Jesus Christ. Getting to know my new-found friend Gwyon kept reminding me that my stereotype of a Christian had been based on pure ignorance. This guy wasn't at all weird. Quite the opposite in fact – he was a great bloke. But in order to cross the second great barrier to faith things couldn't end there. Many people are friends with Christians, or at least know one, so they can affirm that there's nothing weird about following Jesus. Far from it; it proves itself to be a rich source of life for the Christian. Some in this situation find themselves gaining increasing respect for Christians and Christianity. **I know many who say things like, 'I'll have nothing said against Christianity. One of my best friends/ parents/teachers/coaches is a Christian and it really**

Believing in Jesus is neither weird nor irrelevant

makes a difference to their lives.' They've overcome the first barrier but the second one isn't tumbling just yet . . .

It only starts to be overcome when you find yourself thinking 'If Jesus can make that kind of difference to my friend who I admire so much, could he perhaps change my life too?' That word 'perhaps' is the key turning point. It's at this stage that the second barrier to faith begins to wobble. It's the comprehension and emerging hope of the possibility that Jesus might, just might, be interested in me as well as my friend. There are the first stirrings of spiritual hunger and thirst. Respect is now a given, but it's developed into a personal hope. As a person begins to see the second barrier fall their experience can be a combination of wonder, excitement and fear.

The wonder is that God might care about me. Me! The excitement is that perhaps **He understands my dreams, my hopes in a way that no one else in the world can**. What potential. Such stirrings are incredible experiences. But at the same time they often, and understandably, provoke fear. As a person is drawn towards Jesus, as He becomes more personal, it becomes possible to ask the question, 'What will He want from me?' Ideals are fine, but they aren't always practical. However, now there is the possibility that someone might be willing to help you live out your ideals. In order to do so though, you would have to face the truth about yourself. You'd have to expose the fact that for all your idealism, your life has aspects that starkly contradict your dreams – those things would have

One of my best friends is a Christian and it really makes a difference

but it's surely irrelevant?

to go if you were to become the man or woman you dream of being. Could you bear this? What would be the cost? How much would have to go? Are you willing to sacrifice the shadow to bask in the sunlight?

The closing exchange of the story shows us that Jesus was initiating the process of navigating one final barrier in Nathanael's move towards faith in Him – one without which the process would be incomplete.

The wonder is that God might care about me

The truth, the whole truth and nothing but the truth

Jesus said, "You believe because I told you I saw you under the fig-tree. You shall see greater things than that." He then added, "I tell you the truth, you shall see heaven open, and the angels of God ascending and descending on the Son of Man."

Jesus replies to Nathanael's extremely enthusiastic conclusion with the most angular of comments. On first reading it barely fits. Nathanael now understands that Christianity is neither weird nor irrelevant. But there remains, for Jesus, one crucial issue. Nathanael has to understand that **Christianity insists on facing the truth, the whole truth and nothing but the truth**. Nathanael is so thrilled that this stranger knows his hopes and dreams that he has stopped short of all that he needs in order to understand the heart of Christianity. Nathanael's excitement has focused his attention on one area, his felt need to have someone empathise with him at the most intimate level of his idealistic dreams. For Jesus, however, that is insufficient. He is concerned with our expressed needs, but He is more concerned with ensuring we face the truth about our real needs and how they can, and must, be dealt with.

There are so many 'everyday things' in life that can give us comfort and meet some of our desires. Friends at their best are marvellous. They cheer us up and make us feel valued. A nice meal when we're hungry or a good sleep when we're really tired can be so valuable, not least enjoyable. From my point of view, playing a game of football usually means forgetting everything else in the world for an hour and a half. As soon as the whistle blows to kick off, my whole focus is on what's going on within that large green rectangle with twenty-two men, one ball and two smaller white rectangles that the ball is meant to pass between. I love it! Whatever issues I face in everyday life, all the concerns and anxieties, just disappear.

There are religious ways of meeting some of these felt needs too. All religious groups offer to meet our needs for identity, meaning, value and purpose. And it would be churlish and futile for a Christian to even attempt to deny that many and varied groups do achieve this! There are many religious groups who can do a brilliant job of offering community to the lonely, a sense of purpose to the aimless, or of care for the uncared. But that doesn't mean that the basic facts they claim as the foundation of their belief system are actually true, or an accurate reflection of reality. Just because something makes us feel better it doesn't mean it's based on *truth*.

That's why Jesus draws on one more Saturday School lesson for this Jewish lad! *'You believe because I told you I saw you under the fig tree. You shall see greater things than that.' 'You shall see heaven open, and the angels of God ascending and descending upon the Son of Man.'*[16] Can you see Jesus' point? Nathanael, have you changed your mind so dramatically just because I told you I know that you're an idealist? Man, that's nothing. To prove it, Jesus then alludes to another lesson from the Jewish Bible, and so continues in the very language and culture that would have made much sense to Nathanael.

As soon as Jesus mentioned 'angels ascending and descending' Nathanael would have identified the story as being that of Jacob, as found in Genesis chapter 28. The context of the story is that Jacob, who's a real mummy's boy, has with his mother's help, deceived his elder brother and elderly father into giving him, the younger son, the inheritance that should have belonged to his older brother, Esau. As you can imagine, Esau is none too pleased and so Jacob, with his mother's help, devises an excuse to leave home and so avoid his brother's revenge. As he makes his getaway he naturally has to rest and as he falls asleep one night he has a dream in which there is a stairway from heaven to earth, ending right at the spot where he's resting. What is the meaning of the dream? It's this: that God will never stop pursuing Jacob, whatever he's done and however far he tries to run. Instead, God wants Jacob to be aware that God *does* know about his wickedness, that it can't be covered up. He must face up to his deeds and put himself right with his brother, father and his God.

Can you guess the point of Jesus allusion? Jesus is letting Nathanael know that though he is an idealist who yearns for a right relationship with God personally and for a better world to live in this does not mean that he does not share some of the characteristics of Jacob and indeed of Everyman. **Nathanael is a mixture of Jekyll and Hyde, Beauty and the Beast. He yearns for the world to be a better place and yet at the same time he's the man who in part behaves so that the very opposite is inevitable**.

Jesus is saying, in effect: Nathanael, face it! Your idealism is deeply tinged with self-centredness and so it is totally unacceptable to God. You have a touch of the Jacob's about you. Please face up to it. God cares for you, your dreams and your hopes and you feel these desires keenly. But don't miss the crucial point that God is also very aware that there are parts of your character that He sees as unacceptable.

Jesus is reminding Nathanael that the God of the Bible is both a loving and a holy God. He loves the world but equally His perfection and hatred of wrong attitudes and deeds mean that He must judge all who rebel against His perfect way and so against Him. He is a God of absolute and unconditional love, but equally fair and just.

Nathanael needs to acknowledge that this is true. Once he does he will begin to understand why he had to see 'heaven open'.[17] Within three short years Jesus would go to His death on a Roman cross. He would do so on behalf of all who have fallen short of the holy God's standards, even though they deserve nothing less than His judgment. Jesus would take the judgment that all rebels against God

[17] v51

deserve, and that includes even such decent idealists as Nathanael.

That's the truth, the whole truth and nothing but the truth of why Jesus came. **Heaven is torn open so that the creator of the universe could enter the world He had made and bring reconciliation with us, the rebels**. Indeed, someone once called God 'the hound of heaven', the one who will seek you out and find you. And this is precisely what was happening before Philip and Nathanael's eyes. Jesus of Nazareth had been promised by Moses in the law and also by the prophets. The ruler of heaven had left His throne to come into this broken world in order to rescue the wasters. He had come to end His life on a Roman cross, facing the most horrible of deaths devised by a human being. Why? Because all idealists have souls that mix Beauty with the Beast of rebellion against God.

This truth is central to understanding Jesus, and Nathanael could not be allowed to receive a salvation that fell short of the whole package. **Christianity isn't just non-weird and relevant to our daily lives; it is also based on the truth about this world**. God made us yet we are rebels and therefore under His judgment. He is our rescuer by Jesus' death on the cross and He proves He's the king by coming back to life three days after dying. He will come again to judge the living and the dead. Eternal life comes only through trusting in him for our rescue.

Christianity is based on the truth about this world

These are the truth claims of the Christian faith and Jesus introduces these issues into the dialogue because faith must be reasonable as well as intimate, intelligible as well as inspiring.

It took me some time to cross this last barrier. I left Llanelli to study in Cardiff at the age of eighteen. I thought I might have got away from Gwyon. OK, he wasn't weird, nor was his faith irrelevant to him and I could see that it might be relevant to me too. But, as I often informed him in my final year before leaving home, it most certainly couldn't be true. I didn't even believe in God.

For the next three years my postman in Cardiff built some big biceps and my housemates started getting used to a regular early alarm as he pushed parcels the size and weight of the Argos catalogue through our letterbox. When Gwyon Jenkins wrote to defend the truth of the claims of Jesus Christ as found in the Bible, he was thorough. Really thorough. We discussed everything. Could you prove the existence of God? Is there evidence for the resurrection of Jesus? Why would a good God allow suffering? What about other religions? You think of it, we discussed it – or rather I discussed it and he spent hours researching and writing the answer – resulting in an increasingly muscular postman at my end.

In due course he covered every base that I could think of. I concluded that the Christian faith was not weird, irrelevant or untrue; indeed that it was intellectually reasonable as well as emotionally satisfying. I came to the conclusion that to trust in Christ as the ruler of the world and as my rescuer at the cross was the inevitable and only thing to do.

We trust that this was the case for Nathanael* at the conclusion of this story, though we are not told explicitly.

So what about you? Meeting and getting to know Gwyon started the process of overcoming three barriers to faith that have brought me to the most important relationship in the universe, one of forgiveness of my rebellion against my creator and of a restored relationship that, having begun, will last for eternity. Where would you plot yourself in relation to these barriers?

I'm sure you wouldn't have got this far if you still thought Christianity weird or indeed irrelevant. On having trusting Christian friends, many people stall at the question of truth. If you aren't convinced please don't stop considering these issues until you have looked closely at the Bible and the claims of Christ. If you have read this far and know enough about the claims of Christ to trust them, what are you waiting for? It's not weird, nor irrelevant, nor untrue: so it's for you.

Say sorry to God today for being a rebel who's incapable of living consistently with your ideals and thank Him that He sent His son Jesus Christ to die on a cross to take the

*Also known as the Disciple Bartholomew.

nothing but the truth

punishment you deserve and to restore your relationship with Him.

I know you're frightened that you will then turn into a weirdo too. But that's how Christianity has grown for two thousand years. Philip to Nathanael, one mate to another. Nathanael to his mate; Gwyon to Graham, Graham to his mate; your mate to you, you to your mate! The weird barrier falls as one friend talks to another and the cycle continues.

Jesus promises to hear anyone who calls out to Him – why not, even right now, ask Him to forgive you, change you and come and live within you.

Jesus promises to hear anyone who calls out to Him

Further Information

If as a result of reading this book you would like more information about how you can become a Christian, or would like help living your new life as a Christian write to the Series Editor at the address below. We would love to hear from you.

Exploring Christianity, c/o Authentic Media
9 Holdom Avenue, Bletchley, Milton Keynes MK1 1QR

Further Reading

Answers to Tough Questions, Josh McDowell and Don Stewart (Milton Keynes: Authentic Media, 2006)

Christianity Explored, Rico Tice and Barry Cooper (Surrey: The Good Book Company, 2005)

Fresh Start, J.C. Chapman (London: Hodder and Stoughton, 1986)

Real Lives, D.J. Carswell (Milton Keynes: Authentic Media, 2001, reprinted)

Turning Points, Vaughan Roberts (Milton Keynes: Authentic Media, 1999, reprinted)

Uncovered, Jonathan Carswell (Milton Keynes: Authentic Media, 2005, reprinted)

Uncovering the World, Jonathan Carswell (Milton Keynes: Authentic Media, 2006)

Why Believe? Roger Carswell (Milton Keynes: Authentic Media, 2000, reprinted)

Why Should God Bother with Me? Simon Austen (Tain: Christian Focus, 2002)

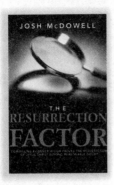

The Resurrection Factor
by Josh McDowell

If Jesus Christ didn't rise from the dead, the Christian faith is worthless!

Can the resurrection be proved beyond any reasonable doubt?

Over thirteen years, Josh McDowell has extensively researched the historical evidence concerning the resurrection of Jesus Christ. Here in his comprehensive study you will discover:

What authenticates the truth of any historical event

The extreme security precautions taken at the tomb of Jesus of Nazareth

How to answer the theories advanced by sceptics to explain away the empty tomb

The incredible implications of the resurrection to life in the twenty-first century

Read with an open mind this book can bring new conviction, fresh purpose and extraordinary joy to your life.

Josh McDowell is a world authority on Christian apologetics and is an international speaker for Campus Crusade for Christ. He is the author of numerous books including *Evidence that Demands a Verdict*, *His Image, My Image* and *Beyond Belief to Convictions*.

ISBN: 978-185078-640-5

*Available on **www.authenticmedia.co.uk**
or from your local Christian bookshop*

Distinctives
by Vaughan Roberts

Daring to be different in a different world

In a fresh and readable style Vaughan Roberts issues a challenging call to Christians to live out their faith. We should be different from the world around us – Christian distinctives should set us apart in how we live, think, act and speak.

Targetting difficult but crucial areas such as our attitude to money and possessions, sexuality, contentment, relativism and service, this is holiness in the tradition of J.C. Ryle for the contemporary generation. Roberts helps us to consider how we are to respond biblically to the temptations and pitfalls surrounding us – giving what we cannot keep, to gain what we cannot lose.

Will you take up the challenge?

Will you dare to be different?

ISBN: 978-185078-331-2

*Available on **www.authenticmedia.co.uk**
or from your local Christian bookshop*

Real Lives
by D.J. Carswell

'You are on a train; you look at the people around you. Someone hides behind a newspaper. Another dozes; a young man nods to the beat from his iPod. A baby cries further along the carriage and a table of football fans celebrate an away victory over a few cans of lager. Someone's mobile goes off; a student sitting next to you sends a text message. Eavesdropping on the conversations, you catch soundbites from those around you. Who exactly are they, you wonder?'

Real people

All different

Everyone with a life story

Real lives

In *Real Lives* you will meet, among others . . . a famous footballer . . . a sophisticated lady from South Africa . . . an Olympic athlete . . . a backpacker exploring the States . . . a Brahmin from India . . . a young, abused girl . . . the greatest man in history who was a child refugee . . . and the author's own story of a changed life.

ISBN: 978-185078-412-8

Available on www.authenticmedia.co.uk or from your local Christian bookshop